Panama

by Heather Adamson

BELLWETHER MEDIA • MINNEAPOLIS, MN

BLASTOFF!
5
READERS

Note to Librarians, Teachers, and Parents:

Blastoff! Readers are carefully developed by literacy experts and combine standards-based content with developmentally appropriate text.

Level 1 provides the most support through repetition of high-frequency words, light text, predictable sentence patterns, and strong visual support.

Level 2 offers early readers a bit more challenge through varied simple sentences, increased text load, and less repetition of high-frequency words.

Level 3 advances early-fluent readers toward fluency through increased text and concept load, less reliance on visuals, longer sentences, and more literary language.

Level 4 builds reading stamina by providing more text per page, increased use of punctuation, greater variation in sentence patterns, and increasingly challenging vocabulary.

Level 5 encourages children to move from "learning to read" to "reading to learn" by providing even more text, varied writing styles, and less familiar topics.

Whichever book is right for your reader, Blastoff! Readers are the perfect books to build confidence and encourage a love of reading that will last a lifetime!

This edition first published in 2016 by Bellwether Media, Inc.

No part of this publication may be reproduced in whole or in part without written permission of the publisher. For information regarding permission, write to Bellwether Media, Inc., Attention: Permissions Department, 5357 Penn Avenue South, Minneapolis, MN 55419.

Library of Congress Cataloging-in-Publication Data

Names: Adamson, Heather, 1974- author.
Title: Panama / by Heather Adamson.
Description: Minneapolis, MN : Bellwether Media, Inc., 2016. | Series:
    Blastoff! Readers: Exploring Countries | Includes bibliographical
    references and index. | Audience: Ages 7-12.
Identifiers: LCCN 2015029354 | ISBN 9781626173453 (hardcover : alk. paper)
Subjects: LCSH: Panama–Juvenile literature.
Classification: LCC F1563.2 .A33 2016 | DDC 972.87–dc23
LC record available at http://lccn.loc.gov/2015029354

Printed in the United States of America, North Mankato, MN.

Contents

Costa Rica

N
W   E
S

Panama is the bridge of the Americas. The country is a narrow, S-shaped **isthmus** connecting North and South America. Costa Rica borders Panama's west and Colombia its east. Its northern border bends around the Caribbean Sea. The Pacific Ocean lines Panama's southern edge.

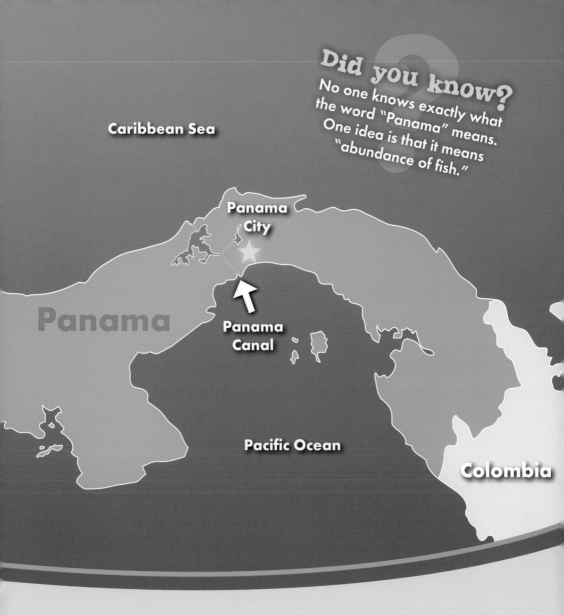

Caribbean Sea

Did you know?
No one knows exactly what the word "Panama" means. One idea is that it means "abundance of fish."

Panama
City

Panama

Panama
Canal

Pacific Ocean

Colombia

This small country covers just 29,120 square miles
(75,420 square kilometers). It is slightly smaller
than the U.S. state of Maine. Panama City is both
the capital and largest city. It sits near the Panama
Canal. This large waterway connects the Atlantic
and Pacific Oceans. It has brought travelers
from around the world to settle in Panama.

Did you know?

Panama's climate differs depending on which side of the mountains you are on. The Caribbean coast gets a lot of rain. The Pacific coast is drier.

Tabasara Mountains

Even though it is small, Panama has a variety of landforms. Mountains form a line across most of the middle of Panama. The highest point, Volcán Barú, is in the Tabasara Mountains. Many short rivers run down the mountains to shores. **Rain forests** cover much of the land. **Plains** and lowlands form around the coasts. Ocean waves crash against Panama's islands and **peninsulas**.

Panama has a **tropical** climate. It has a rainy and a dry season. Temperatures are usually warm all year, at around 70 to 90 degrees Fahrenheit (21 to 32 degrees Celsius).

! fun fact

One of Panama's many rain forests is within Panama City limits.

The Darién Gap may be the most dangerous place to travel in the world. This stretch of swampy, thick jungle is roughly 60 to 100 miles (100 to 160 kilometers) wide. It forms the border between Central America and South America. There are no roads through the jungle. Traveling the rough ground requires great hiking skills and a canoe. Still, there are a few **native** tribes that live in the forest.

Jaguars, caimans, vipers, fire ants, and herds of peccaries are a few of the wild animals roaming the area. The jungle also makes a good hideout for criminals. Because of the dangers, the government allows few people into the area.

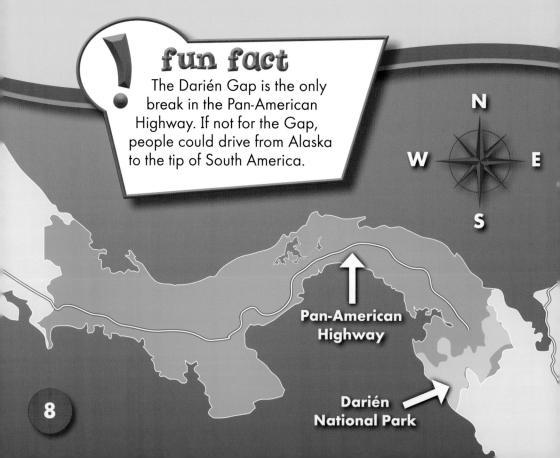

fun fact

The Darién Gap is the only break in the Pan-American Highway. If not for the Gap, people could drive from Alaska to the tip of South America.

N
W   E
S

Pan-American
Highway

Darién
National Park

Did you know?

The Darién Gap has been important in stopping the spread of tropical diseases. Sicknesses from one continent have not been able to spread to the other because travel is limited.

Did you know?
Panamanian golden frogs are unique to Panama. The frogs use a foot language. They lift and wave their feet to communicate with other frogs.

An amazing amount of wildlife fits within Panama's small area. Delicate orchids grow in the rain forests along with guava and papaya trees. Panama's trees also make it one of the best places for bird-watching. Parrots, toucans, and tanagers are known for their colors. The national bird is the harpy eagle, a powerful **raptor**.

harpy eagle

howler monkey

beetle

! fun fact

In Panama, scientists found more than 950 different kinds of beetles living on just one tree!

Many rare animals also live in Panama. Howler monkeys, sloths, tamarins, tapirs, golden frogs, and capybaras call this country home. Panama's two coasts also host five kinds of sea turtles during nesting season. Just off shore, **coral reefs** and small islands support many fish and sea creatures.

Did you know?
Molas are traditional clothing and art in Panama. Brightly colored pieces of raised fabric are sewn on shirts and purses.

More than 3.6 million people live in Panama. Many of Panama's people can trace their backgrounds to more than one culture. Citizens who have native and European backgrounds are called *mestizos*. They make up the largest population group. Native peoples still live in Panama as well. The Guaymí, Kuna, and Embera groups are the largest.

Spanish is Panama's official language. However, many people in Panama speak more than one language. The main religion in Panama is Roman Catholicism, though some practice other forms of Christianity.

Speak Spanish!

English	Spanish	How to say it
hello	hola	OH-lah
good-bye	adiós	ah-dee-OHS
yes	sí	SEE
no	no	NOH
please	por favor	POHR fah-VOR
thank you	gracias	GRAH-see-uhs
friend (male)	amigo	ah-MEE-goh
friend (female)	amiga	ah-MEE-gah

Most people in Panama live or work by the canal. About half of Panama's population lives in or around Panama City. The city shows off its mixed culture in **traditional** and **urban** music, foods, and clothing styles. In the city, people live in houses and apartments. They drive or take a bus to work.

About one in every three Panamanians lives in a **rural** area. People living out in the country have small homes. Many live on ranches or farms. Some families still live in small **cabanas** with thatched roofs. People in the country may travel to work. They walk or take a bus.

Where People Live in Panama

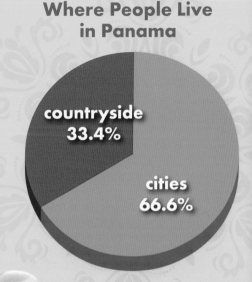

countryside
33.4%

cities
66.6%

fun fact

The famous "Panama hat" is not actually from Panama. These straw hats are made in Ecuador.

cabana

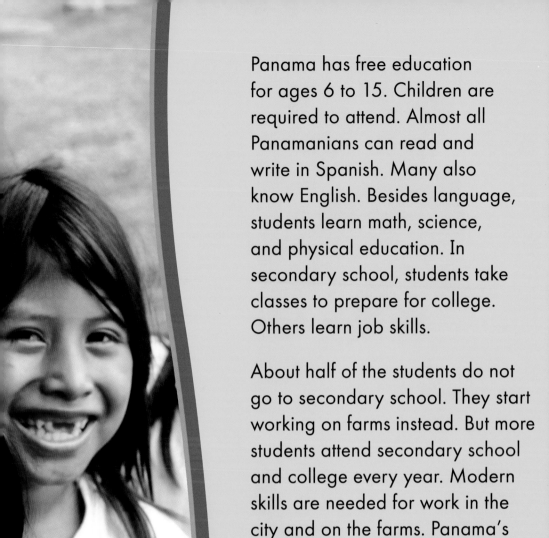

Panama has free education for ages 6 to 15. Children are required to attend. Almost all Panamanians can read and write in Spanish. Many also know English. Besides language, students learn math, science, and physical education. In secondary school, students take classes to prepare for college. Others learn job skills.

About half of the students do not go to secondary school. They start working on farms instead. But more students attend secondary school and college every year. Modern skills are needed for work in the city and on the farms. Panama's education system continues to improve with the times.

fun fact

The school year in Panama goes from the end of February to the end of December.

Where People Work in Panama

manufacturing 18.6%

services 64.4%

farming 17%

In the city, people work all kinds of **service jobs**. Doctors and teachers keep the city going. Hotels and tour companies provide services for **tourists**. Many people in the city **manufacture** food products and construction materials. Workers are also needed to keep the Panama Canal running smoothly.

Outside of the city, jobs are usually in agriculture. Bananas are a main crop. Workers also tend to sugarcane, corn, rice, and coffee beans. Herders and ranchers care for animals. Farmers used to just grow enough food for their families. Now many crops and livestock are sold. Even the native people bring baskets and clothes to sell in the city.

The national sport of Panama is baseball, but the people also love soccer. Locals regularly gather together to watch baseball and soccer matches on TV. Panama is also known for its music and dancing. Salsa, jazz, reggae, and rock-and-roll are all popular in Panama. People love to go out to concerts or to dance clubs.

fun fact

The *tamborito* is a Panamanian folk dance. The dancers wear traditional costumes and perform for large audiences.

Another top activity is going to the beach. Snorkeling, fishing, surfing, and swimming are just some of Panama's many water sports. Panamanians often spend their vacations at the shore.

sancocho

Food in Panama is a mix of Latin American, African, Caribbean, and native flavors. Fried or baked **plantains** and rice and beans are always popular. *Arepas* are flatbread sandwiches filled with things like cheese and eggs. They are often made from cornmeal. *Ceviche* is a dish of marinated seafood and onions. The flavorful chicken stew, *sancocho*, is the national dish. For dessert, Panamanians might eat *tres leches* cake or flan custard.

Many choices of fresh fruit juice can be found in Panama. Watermelon and pineapple are favorites. People sip *pipa* from a straw placed directly in a green coconut. Locally grown coffee is served black or with milk.

ceviche

arepa

Panama celebrates many holidays. *Carnaval* is a popular celebration in spring. It involves large concerts, parades, and parties in the streets. Good Friday, Easter, and Christmas are major religious holidays. People attend church and gather for special meals.

There are so many holidays in November that little business gets done. Independence Day from Colombia, Independence Day from Spain, Flag Day, and the Day of the Dead are just a few. Most people have these national holidays off from work. Everyone makes a lot of food and visits friends and families. They also celebrate in the streets with music and dancing.

Independence Day

Carnaval

The Panama Canal is a 50-mile (80-kilometer)
long waterway connecting the Atlantic and Pacific
Oceans. It provides a shorter path than traveling
around South America. Work started on the canal
in the 1880s but was not completed until 1914.
For many years, the United States owned the
canal. Control passed to Panama in 1999.

Did you know?
A large barge could pay as much as $450,000 to pass through the canal.

NS STREAM

Today, about 9,000 people work along the canal. Boats are charged a **toll** to use it. Several **locks** lift and lower boats through. Water is added or drained in each lock to bring boats to the level of the next lock. About 40 barges and ships pass through the canal each day. Panama serves as a gateway for the whole world.

Fast Facts About Panama

Panama's Flag

Panama's flag is made up of four equal rectangles. Blue and red stand for the country's two main political parties. White represents peace between them. The blue star is for purity and honesty. The red star stands for the law.

Official Name: Republic of Panama

Area: 29,120 square miles (75,420 square kilometers); Panama is the 118th largest country in the world.

Capital City:	Panama City
Important Cities:	San Miguelito, Tocumen, Colón
Population:	3,657,024 (July 2015)
Official Language:	Spanish
National Holiday:	Independence Day (November 3)
Religions:	Catholic (85%), Protestant (15%)
Major Industries:	operating the Panama Canal, sugar milling, farming, tourism, construction
Natural Resources:	fish, timber, clay, limestone, salt
Manufactured Products:	food products, oil, natural gas, clothing, leather
Farm Products:	bananas, rice, corn, coffee beans, sugarcane
Unit of Money:	the balboa; the balboa is equal to the U.S. dollar, which is also accepted as money.

Glossary

cabanas—small, lightweight shacks or buildings built from wood or sugarcane stalks with thatched roofs

canal—a waterway that is built to connect two larger bodies of water

coral reefs—structures made of coral that usually grow in shallow seawater

isthmus—a narrow strip of land that connects two larger pieces of land; an isthmus lies between two bodies of water.

locks—compartments in canals with gates on either end; locks are used to raise or lower boats as they pass from level to level.

manufacture—to use a machine to make products

native—originally from a specific place

peninsulas—sections of land that extend out from a larger piece of land and are almost completely surrounded by water

plains—large areas of flat land

plantains—a type of banana that is less sweet and usually cooked

rain forests—thick, green forests that receive a lot of rain

raptor—a large bird of prey

rural—relating to the countryside

service jobs—jobs that perform tasks for people or businesses

toll—a charge or tax paid for using a road, bridge, or canal

tourists—people who travel to visit another place

traditional—relating to a custom, idea, or belief handed down from one generation to the next

tropical—part of the tropics; the tropics is a hot, rainy region near the equator.

urban—relating to cities and city life

To Learn More

AT THE LIBRARY

Blashfield, Jean F. *Panama*. New York, N.Y.:
Children's Press, 2015.

Hinman, Bonnie. *We Visit Panama*. Hockessin, Del.:
Mitchell Lane, 2010.

Miller, Heather. *The Panama Canal*. Chicago, Ill.:
Norwood House Press, 2014.

ON THE WEB

Learning more about Panama
is as easy as 1, 2, 3.

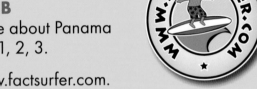

1. Go to www.factsurfer.com.

2. Enter "Panama" into the search box.

3. Click the "Surf" button and you will see a list of
   related web sites.

With factsurfer.com, finding more information is just
a click away.

Index

The images in this book are reproduced through the courtesy of: Picturemakersllc, front cover; Icon design, front cover (flag), p. 28; Heeb Christian/ Glow Images, p. 6; Hannes Vos, p. 7; Rafal Cichawa, p. 9; david tipling/ Alamy, p. 10; MarcusVDT, p. 11 (top); Elliotte Rusty Harold, p. 11 (middle); Foxyjoshi, p. 11 (bottom); Danita Delimont/ Alamy, p. 12; Massimo Ripani/ Grand Tour/ Corbis, p. 14; Gualberto Becerra, pp. 15 (top), 24; Rob Crandall, p. 15 (bottom); Visual&Written SL/ Alamy, p. 16; Joel Carillet, p. 18; SuperStock/ Glow Images, p. 19 (left); Alfredo Maiquez/ Alamy, p. 19 (right); Jose Angel Murillo/ Alamy, p. 20; Vilainecrevette, p. 21; Humberto Olarte Cupas/ Alamy, p. 22; age fotostock/ SuperStock/ Alamy, pp. 23 (left), 26-27; REDAV, p. 23 (right); epa european pressphoto agency b.v./ Alamy, p. 25; Martin Otero, p. 29 (top); nimon, p. 29 (bottom).